ABBA OUR FATHER

Father of the Human Family

10 Reasons Why

www.FatherFeast.com

SUMMARY

www.FatherFeast.com

"The Our Father begins with a great consolation: we are allowed to say "Father." This one word contains the whole history of redemption."[1]

Reinhold Schneider, Poet

"It is sad that in the whole liturgical year there isn't a feast dedicated to the Father, that in the whole Missal there isn't even a votive Mass in His honour. Come to think of it, it's very strange; there are many feasts dedicated to Jesus the Son; there is a feast of the Holy Spirit; there are many feasts dedicated to Mary... There isn't a single feast dedicated to the Father, *"source and origin of all divinity."* We could almost say that the Father, and no longer the Holy Spirit, is "the unknown divinity."[2]

Raniero Cardinal Cantalamessa, OFM Cap,
Papal Preacher to Popes St. John Paul II, Benedict XVI and Francis

"The absence of a feast dedicated to the Father in the liturgical calendar bears witness to the fact that the worship of the Father still hasn't reached its full development. During the year there are feasts dedicated to Christ in memory of numerous events of the work of salvation, the feast of the Holy Spirit at Pentecost, the feast of the Holy Trinity, the feasts dedicated to Our Lady and those dedicated to numerous saints. However, there is no particular feast dedicated to the Father: Unlike the other two divine persons, the Father isn't celebrated with a feast dedicated only to Him."[3]
Jean Galot, S.J., Professor, Pontifical Gregorian University (1972-2008)

"The liturgical cycle enables Christians to relive the unfolding of the mystery of salvation in its various stages and in its most important events. The Father is at the origin and at the conclusion of the mystery. The entire work of sanctification results from his paternal love and tends to produce, as its ultimate fruit, the return of humankind to him. His paternal role, which is absolutely primordial and decisive, deserves to be recognized and venerated by a special feast."[4]

Jean Galot, S.J.

SUMMARY

In the fullness of time, the biblical narrative; the logic of the liturgy; patristic, conciliar and papal teaching; doctrinal development; anthropological breakthroughs; ecumenical and inter-religious solidarity; and the flow of salvation history have led to a growing recognition of the singular role of God the Father. For centuries, it has been the hope and the prayer of many that this great discovery will be translated into the Church's declaration and celebration of a Feast of Abba our Father, the Father of the Human Family.

As a welcome example, for nearly two hundred years, Brazil, the world's largest Catholic country, has celebrated the Feast of the Divine Eternal Father on the first Sunday of July, now at the Basilica of the Divine Eternal Father in the pilgrimage city of Trindade, not too far from the national capital Brasília.

Here are ten considerations that call for extending a feast of the Father – in celebration of his role in the salvific order – to the universal Church.

#1 **Biblical**	"A son honors his father … If, then, I am a father, **where is the honor due to me**? …So says the LORD of hosts to you." (*Malachi* 1:6) "**I will be a father to you**, and you shall be sons and daughters to me, says the Lord Almighty." (2 *Corinthians* 6:18) "But the hour is coming, and is now here, when **true worshipers will worship the Father** in Spirit and truth; *and indeed the Father seeks such people to worship him.*" (*John* 4:23) *Cardinal Pietro Parolin* – "God's fatherhood is the lens that enables us to understand everything that Jesus says and does in the Gospels: every action and every word of the Son points to the primacy of the one he calls 'my Father.'"
#2 **Liturgical**	*Catechism of the Catholic Church* – "The Eucharist is a sacrifice of thanksgiving to the Father, a blessing by which the Church expresses her gratitude to God for all his benefits, for all that he has accomplished through creation, redemption, and sanctification." *Jean Galot*, S.J. – "We note this paradox: the Father, who is the origin of the whole work of salvation and has instituted the entire foundation of the liturgy, is not personally celebrated by this liturgy. He who has the right to be celebrated before the other persons is not honored with a particular feast."
#3 **Patristic**	*St. Irenaeus of Lyons* (140-202) – "There is one God the Father, who is above all and through all and in all." *St Augustine* (354-430) – "'The Father is the principle of all divinity or, to be more precise, of the deity, because he does not take his origin from anything else. He has no one from whom he has his being or from whom he proceeds, but it is by him that the Son is begotten and from him that the Holy Spirit proceeds." *Pontifical Council for Promoting Christian Unity* – "The Father alone is the principle without principle of the two other persons of the Trinity, the sole source of the Son and of the Holy Spirit. … The two traditions [of East and West] recognize that the 'monarchy of the Father' implies that the Father is the sole Trinitarian Cause or Principle of the Son and the Holy Spirit."

#4 Conciliar	*Councils of Nicaea (325) and Constantinople (381)* – "We believe in one God, the father almighty, maker of heaven and earth and of all things visible and invisible." *Council of Florence (1438-1445)* – The Father is "the source and principle of all deity, that is of the Son and of the holy Spirit." *Catechism of the Council of Trent (1545-1563)* – "How great is the fecundity of the Father, who contemplating and understanding Himself, begot the Son like and equal to Himself, how a love of charity in both, entirely the same and equal, which is the Holy Ghost, proceeding from the Father and the Son, connects the begetter and the begotten by an eternal and indissoluble bond." *Lumen Gentium, Second Vatican Council (1962-1965)* – "The eternal Father, by a free and hidden plan of His own wisdom and goodness, created the whole world. His plan was to raise men to a participation of the divine life. … The Son, therefore, came, sent by the Father. It was in Him, before the foundation of the world, that the Father chose us and predestined us to become adopted sons, for in Him it pleased the Father to re-establish all things. … When the work which the Father gave the Son to do on earth was accomplished, the Holy Spirit was sent on the day of Pentecost in order that He might continually sanctify the Church, and thus, all those who believe would have access through Christ in one Spirit to the Father."
#5 Papal	*Pope St. John Paul II* – "It is the Father who is the absolute principle in Trinitarian life, the one who has no origin and from whom the divine life flows. The unity of the three Persons is a sharing in the one divine essence, but in the dynamism of reciprocal relations that have their source and foundation in the Father." *Pope St. John Paul II* – "The whole of the Christian life is like a great pilgrimage to the house of the Father, whose unconditional love for every human creature, especially for the "prodigal son", we discover anew each day."

	Pope Benedict XVI – "God is our Father, giving us his Son; God is our Father, pardoning our sin and bringing us to joy in everlasting life; God is our Father, giving us the Spirit that makes us sons and enables us to call him, in truth "Abba, Father!" (cf. Rom 8:15). It is for this reason that Jesus, teaching us to pray, invites us to say "Our Father" (Mt 6:9-13; cf. Lk 11:2-4). Consequently God's fatherhood is infinite love, tenderness that bends over us, frail children, in need of everything." *Pope Benedict XVI* – "The Spirit is also the energy which transforms the heart of the ecclesial community, so that it becomes a witness before the world to the love of the Father, who wishes to make humanity a single family in his Son." Benedict XVI, Deus Caritas Est, "God Is Love," 2006 *Pope Francis* – "The first step of every Christian prayer is the entry into a mystery, that of the fatherhood of God. … Either you enter into the mystery, in the awareness that God is your Father, or you do not pray. … The hunger for love that we all feel is not a yearning for something nonexistent: it is instead an invitation to know God who is father." *Pope Francis* – "We can say that Christian prayer arises from the courage to address God with the name 'Father'."
#6 **Theological**	The Bible is a story of humanity turning away from the Father and then, through his initiative, returning to him. "God so loved the world that he gave his only Son, so that everyone who believes in him might not perish but might have eternal life." (*John* 3:16) As proof that you are children, God sent the Spirit of his Son into our hearts, crying out, 'Abba, Father!'" (*Galatians* 4:6) *Jean Galot* – "Precisely, because He is the initiator of all the work of salvation and the ultimate end of the journey of redeemed humanity, the Father should be celebrated. The liturgy must follow the essential movement which characterizes the journey and the worship of Christ, which goes from the Father to the Father."

#7 **Anthropological**	*Cardinal Ratzinger* – "The crisis of fatherhood we are living today is an element, perhaps the most important, threatening man in his humanity. The dissolution of fatherhood and motherhood is linked to the dissolution of our being sons and daughters." *Paul Vitz* – "The psychological significance of the fatherhood of God helps to maintain the complementary understanding of the sexes, for both men and women." *Benedict Ashley* – "The term 'Father' used of God in no way implies that he is male, but only that as our father gave us life and loves and cares for us, so does God." *Janet Soskice Smith* – "Biblical authors use many gendered terms, not because they are interested in sex but because they are very interested in kinship and kinship terms which, in most natural languages, are gendered. Kinship titles are titles of intimacy, of blood relation."
#8 **Millennial**	The year-by-year calendar laid out for the Jubilee year of 2000 – the Year of the Son, then the Holy Spirit and, finally, the Father – may be seen to have a counterpart in the three Christian millennia. We "discovered" the full identity of the Son in the first millennium through its Seven Ecumenical Councils, in the second we came to recognize the action of the Holy Spirit and now, in the third millennium, we have the opportunity to acknowledge the Father's role in salvation history by celebrating a Feast in his honor and consecrating the world to him. Such a present-day consecration of the world to the Father is appropriate given Pope Leo XIII's consecration of the world to the Son (1899) and then to the Holy Spirit (1901). It would be fitting to complete these consecrations with a consecration of the world to the Father.

#9 **Ecumenical**	*Jean Galot* – "Instituting a feast in honor of God our Father would certainly be a step in the direction of the reunion of Christians. This unifying role is at the heart of our veneration of God our Father: Christians cannot pray to their heavenly Father without by that very fact being more closely united among themselves of the same spiritual family. The feast would be a symbol of Christian unity and a powerful impetus toward reconciliation." *Raniero Cantalamessa* – "Christians would certainly give great joy to the risen Lord if they were able to accomplish this project 'ecumenically', that is, reaching an agreement with all the Churches who accept it in order to celebrate, with one accord, the feast of the Father on the same day." *Unitatis Redintegratio, Vatican II* – "The Lord of Ages," the Father, "has been rousing divided Christians to remorse over their divisions and to a longing for unity." A feast for the Father, whom Christians of every denomination invoke in the Lord's prayer, would lend a unique impetus to their reaching the end-point prayed for by their Savior where "they all would be one." A feast for the Father will also mark an irrevocable milestone in inter-religious relations. *Nostra Aetate, Vatican II* – "From ancient times down to the present, there is found among various peoples a certain perception of that hidden power which hovers over the course of things and over the events of human history; at times some indeed have come to the recognition of a Supreme Being, or even of a Father." Historian of religion *Mircea Eliade* – "The most popular prayer in the world is addressed to 'Our Father who art in heaven.' It is possible that man's earliest prayers were addressed to the same heavenly father."

	A feast of the Father would be the one feast that could resonate with the Jewish people in particular. In an unprecedented declaration titled "To Do the Will of Our Father in Heaven: Toward a Partnership between Jews and Christians," Orthodox rabbis from Israel, Europe and the United States said, "We seek to do the will of our Father in Heaven by accepting the hand offered to us by our Christian brothers and sisters. Jews and Christians must work together as partners to address the moral challenges of our era." A feast honoring our Father in Heaven will help cement the Partnership.
#10 **Fruit-full**	All feasts bear fruits. A feast for the Father would bear singular fruits – a living awareness of the Holy Trinity manifested in both liturgical worship and our devotional life; a greater appreciation for the family as a reflection of the divine Family that is the Trinity; a new respect for fatherhood and all parentage for as St. Paul said "every family in heaven and on earth is named" from the Father. The feast will fulfill Jesus' prophecy of the hour when "true worshipers … will worship the Father in Spirit and truth." (*John* 4:23) Through such a feast, the Father will grant "the riches of his glory (…) so that [we] may be filled with all the fullness of God." (*Ephesians* 3:14-17,19)

THE FEAST

Raniero Cantalamessa – "In the teachings of the Church, feasts have always been a privileged means of allowing a particular mystery or event of the history of salvation to penetrate in the lives of the faithful. The knowledge and familiarity of the Holy Spirit certainly wouldn't be so strong without the feast of Pentecost. Feasts are a living catechesis and today there is an urgent need for a catechesis on the Father. Besides its catechetic value, a feast dedicated to the Father would also have, like any other feast, the value of *homologesis*, that is of a public and joyful confession of faith. In fact, feasts are the highest and most solemn form of proclaiming one's faith, because all people participate in it unanimously."

Jean Galot – "A liturgical feast of God the Father should not have the eternal fatherhood within the Trinity as its principal theme. Rather, such a feast should express homage to the fatherhood that the Father has deigned to assume in relation to the members of the human race, homage to his paternal love as it has been manifested in the work of salvation. This is the purpose of the praise that St. Paul offered the Father in the hymn of the Letter to the Ephesians. ...

The real object of the feast, therefore, is the fatherhood of God the Father in relation to [humanity], a fatherhood in which the eternal fatherhood is revealed."

A feast of God the Father has been celebrated officially within the Catholic Church since the 1840s. The Archdiocese of Goiânia in Brazil celebrates the Feast of the Divine Eternal Father annually. Its cathedral sanctuary of the Divine Eternal Father was officially made a Basilica during the pontificate of Benedict XVI. It is the second largest pilgrimage destination in Brazil drawing 3 million pilgrims during the Feast Day novena which begins on the last Friday of June and ends on the first Sunday of July. The current Archbishop of Goiânia was appointed by Pope Francis in 2021 and is Vice-President of the Brazilian Bishops Conference. It is significant indeed that the largest Catholic country in the world, Brazil (123 million Catholics), has a feast celebrating God the Father. The aspiration now is for the extension of this feast – as a feast for God the Father of humankind – to the entire Church.

Also noteworthy is the fact that the Ethiopian Orthodox Church has celebrated a feast of God the Father for centuries.

#1 BIBLICAL

The New Testament shows us that the whole identity and mission of Jesus of Nazareth reflects his filial relationship with the Father. Jesus always addresses God as Father (with the exception of his citation of Psalm 22 on the cross).[1]

As Cardinal Pietro Parolin points out,

To Mary and Joseph, so deeply troubled, Jesus gives a remarkable answer: "Did you not know that I must be in my Father's house?" (Lk 2:49). … It is significant that in Luke's Gospel, those were the first words that Jesus utters. After his silence in the womb of the Virgin, the first word that Luke puts on the lips of Jesus is "Father". It would also be his last word, uttered on the cross: "Father, into your hands I commend my spirit" (Lk 23:46). God's fatherhood is the lens that enables us to understand everything that Jesus says and does in the Gospels: every action and every word of the Son points to the primacy of the one he calls "my Father."

That fatherhood, which becomes prayer in the "Our Father", takes on life in our fraternal relations with one another. The Second Vatican Council saw in human fraternity a most precious fruit of God's fatherhood: "We cannot truly pray to God, the Father of all, unless we treat others as sisters and brothers, for all are created in God's image" (Nostra Aetate, 5).[2]

The Father is "father" because Jesus, as Word, is his infinite-eternal Son, and the Love between Father and Son is such that it bears fruit as Another, the Holy Spirit.

The Father revealed by Jesus was prodigal in his limitless love; closer than any earthly parent and therefore called *Abba* (the affectionate Aramaic expression for one's own father); and, above all, "our" Father meeting all our needs through the protection and provision of his Providence. Henceforth, we cannot see God except as the Father who makes us his adopted children through his Son and in his Holy Spirit. "As proof that you are children, God sent the Spirit of his Son into our hearts, crying out, 'Abba, Father!'" (*Galatians* 4:6).

Already in the Old Testament, we are given glimpses of the Father's love. "When Israel was a child I loved him, out of Egypt I called my son. The more I called them, the farther they went from me, sacrificing to the Baals and burning incense to idols. Yet it was I who taught Ephraim to walk, who took them in my arms; but they did not know that I cared for them. I drew them with human cords, with bands of love; I fostered them like those who raise an infant to their cheeks; I bent down to feed them. … How could I give you up, Ephraim, or deliver you up, Israel?" (*Hosea* 11: 1-4, 8-9)

This same theme is repeated in the New Testament: "**I will be a father to you, and you shall be sons and daughters to me**, says the Lord Almighty." (2 *Corinthians* 6:18)

In both Testaments, we are asked to honor and love the Father. Moses tells the Israelites: "Is this how you repay the LORD, so foolish and unwise a people? **Is he not your father who begot you**, the one who made and established you?" (*Deuteronomy* 32:6)

The prophet Jeremiah receives a poignant Paternal message: "I thought: How I would like to make you my children! So I gave you a pleasant land, the most beautiful heritage among the nations! **You would call me, "My Father," I thought**, and you would never turn away from me. But like a woman faithless to her lover, thus have you been faithless to me." (*Jeremiah* 3:19-20)

In *Malachi*, we read, "Have we not all one father? Has not one God created us?" (*Malachi* 2:10)

This Father must be honored: "A son honors his father … If, then, I am a father, **where is the honor due to me**? …So says the LORD of hosts to you." (*Malachi* 1:6)

Thus, St. Paul tells the Ephesians, "I kneel before the Father, from whom every family in heaven and on earth is named, that he may grant you in accord with the riches of his glory to be strengthened with power through his Spirit in the inner self, and that Christ may dwell in your hearts through faith; (…) so that you may be filled with all the fullness of God." (*Ephesians* 3:14-17,19)

The movement from and to the Father reaches a crescendo in Jesus' stunning declaration in the Gospel of John: **"But the hour is coming, and is now here, when true worshipers will worship the Father in Spirit and truth;** *and indeed the Father seeks such people to worship him."* (*John* 4:23)

Jesus says "It was for this purpose that I came to this hour. Father, glorify your name." (*John* 12:27-8)

God is to be approached as Father. True worship of God is worship of the Father. The Father seeks out those who worship him in Spirit and truth. This is the God revealed by Jesus of Nazareth.

In his exegesis of *John* 4:23, Jean Galot writes,

In saying 'the hour is coming and is now' Jesus demonstrated he was aware of the times in which he was living. It was a moment of radical transformation in worship determined by God's own plan. A new age in the religious history of humankind was dawning. The era of national partisanship in worship, the time of the fathers, was over. …

The time of the Father had come; it was he, the one and only Father, who laid the foundations of universality in worship and adoration.

The worship that was being inaugurated was first of all adoration of God the Father. It was no longer simply veneration of the one God. … Jesus made it clear that authentic worship discerns the Father. The Father is seen as much closer to humankind than the God of sovereign power. The Father calls for an adoration filled with a filial spirit than a spirit of fear. Jesus showed that worship must be a response to the Father's love. …

Worship now assumes a different aspect inasmuch as it is henceforth addressed to the Father. The relationship it implies is no longer merely that of a servant or slave to an all-powerful Master, or of a creature to its Creator, but of a child to his or her Father. Adoration can no longer be burdened with fear and trembling, since it must express a filial devotion. This has resulted in a transformation of the nature and climate of worship. …

The new worship is inspired by the Holy Spirit and is carried out in the truth revealed by Jesus. This Trinitarian dimension, which implies the distinctions among the divine persons, directs worship more clearly to the person of the Father.

If liturgical worship must be directed to the Father, should we not expect to have a yearly celebration of the feast of God the Father? Should not a special feast be dedicated to the Father, so as to draw greater attention to his person and to honor in him what relates specifically to his fatherhood?[2]

Has this happened? Galot replies,

The new worship which Jesus began consists of adoring the Father: and yet there is no day in which this adoration is directed more particularly to the person of the Father.[3]

#2 LITURGICAL

The Eucharist, says the *Catechism of the Catholic Church*, is "the source and summit of the Christian life."[1] The Eucharistic liturgy, the Mass, is directed to the Father. As we read in the *Catechism*, "In the Eucharistic sacrifice the whole of creation loved by God is presented to the Father through the death and the Resurrection of Christ. ... The Eucharist is a sacrifice of thanksgiving to the Father, a blessing by which the Church expresses her gratitude to God for all his benefits, for all that he has accomplished through creation, redemption, and sanctification."[2]

Why a Feast of the Father is Required in Our Worship

"Throughout the New Testament," writes Louis Bouyer, "God, *ho theos*, does not designate the Trinity, even less one or the other of the three persons indifferently, but always and only the Father. ... The same usage is to be found in all the traditional liturgies, and above all in the Roman liturgy, when not obscured by the medievals or the moderns, and found especially in what is the heart of every liturgy: the great eucharistic prayer and, here once again, most prominently in the Roman canon. We must of course hasten to add that this does not prevent both biblical and liturgical texts being perfectly clear on the equal, undivided possession of divinity by the Son and by the Spirit. But it remains true, that in the perspective proper to these texts, the first subject of this divinity is *the Father*, and the Father only."[3]

Galot highlights the liturgical importance of the Father:

The Father intervened with His supreme initiative in all the events of the saving work and He cannot be considered extraneous to the fulfilment of His divine plan of humanity's redemption. He is also the first promoter of the entire liturgy. Precisely, because He is the initiator of all the work of salvation and the ultimate end of the journey of redeemed humanity, the Father should be celebrated. The liturgy must follow the essential movement which characterizes the journey and the worship of Christ, which goes from the Father to the Father.[4]

Cantalamessa points out that "In the teachings of the Church, feasts have always been a privileged means of allowing a particular mystery or event of the history of salvation to penetrate in the lives of the faithful. The knowledge and familiarity of the Holy Spirit certainly wouldn't be so strong without the feast of Pentecost. Feasts are a living catechesis and today there is an urgent need for a catechesis on the Father."[5]

Galot argues that the very infrastructure of the liturgy underlines the urgency of a feast of the Father:

Therefore we note this paradox: the Father, who is the origin of the whole work of salvation and has instituted the entire foundation of the liturgy, is not personally celebrated by this liturgy. He who has the right to be celebrated before the other persons is not honored with a particular feast. … We have observed that the new worship which Jesus began consists of adoring the Father: and yet there is no day in which this adoration is directed more particularly to the person of the Father. This observation is all the more surprising when we see in today's humanity a growing conviction of the importance of fatherhood. Father's day is celebrated in families: many feel the need to recognize the merits of fathers and to thank them. Even Christians, who value the importance of fatherhood along with motherhood, do not venerate with a special feast He who is the source of every fatherhood and every motherhood. [6]

#3 PATRISTIC

The Fathers of the Church considered God the Father in the context of the revelation of the Holy Trinity. They were clear that the Father was the principle of divinity in the Trinity as illustrated in the writings of Fathers from the second to the fifth centuries.

St. Irenaeus of Lyons (140-202)

"There is one God the Father, who is above all and through all and in all. The Father indeed is above all, and He is the Head of Christ. But the Word is through all, and He is the Head of the Church. The Spirit, however, is in us all, and He is the Living Water which the Lord grants to those who rightly believe in Him and love Him and who know that there is one Father, who is above all and through all and in us all."[1]

St. Athanasius (295-373)

"There is a Trinity, holy and perfect, acknowledged as God, in Father, Son and Holy Spirit. …

Whoever believes in the Father knows the Son is in the Father, and the Spirit not outside the Son; and in this way he believes also in the Son and in the Holy Spirit. Since the Godhead of the Trinity is one, It is known out of the one Father. This is the stamp of the

Catholic faith. … It is a Trinity, and in it are Father and Son and Holy Spirit. And there is one God, Father over all and through all and in all, who is blessed unto the ages."[2]

St. Basil the Great (330-379)

"The Son is second in order from the Father, because He is from Him; and in dignity, because the Father is his origin and cause, whereby the Father is his Father, and because it is through the Son that access and approach is had to God the Father. The Son is not, however, second to the Father in nature, because the Godhead is one in each of them, and plainly, too, in the Holy Spirit, even if in order and dignity He is second to the Son, though not in such a way, it is clear, that He were of another nature."[3]

St Augustine (354-430)

"The Father is the principle of all divinity or, to be more precise, of the deity, because he does not take his origin from anything else. He has no one from whom he has his being or from whom he proceeds, but it is by him that the Son is begotten and from him that the Holy Spirit proceeds."[4]

Doctors of the Trinity like St. Thomas Aquinas[5] have emphasized the fact that the Father is the "source" or "fount of the divinity" in the Trinity. Louis Bouyer observes that "Revelation is quite clear on this point: Christian monotheism is neither solely nor primarily that of a divine essence. It is that of the divine monarchy, of the Father, the one principle of divinity as of all that has come from it."[6]

The Churches of East and West agree on the "monarchy of the Father" as noted by the Pontifical Council for Promoting Christian Unity: "The Father alone is the principle without principle of the two other persons of the Trinity, the sole source of the Son and of the Holy Spirit. … The two traditions recognize that the 'monarchy of the Father' implies that the Father is the sole Trinitarian Cause or Principle of the Son and the Holy Spirit."[7]

#4 CONCILIAR

The role of the Father "within" the Trinity and with respect to the divine attributes "appropriated" to him were refined and defined by the Councils of the Church.

The essential doctrines of the Trinity and the Incarnation were the focus of the seven Ecumenical Councils and Creeds of the Church. The earliest Councils, Nicaea and Constantinople, spoke of the Father in this context. Thus, with respect to the Father, the creeds of Nicaea (325) and Constantinople (381) proclaimed, "I believe in one God, the father almighty, maker of heaven and earth and of all things visible and invisible."[1]

Later councils elaborated on the relations and roles of the Three Persons.

The Fourth Lateran Council (1215) said, "We firmly believe and openly confess that there is only one true God, eternal and immense, omnipotent, unchangeable, incomprehensible, and ineffable, Father, Son, and Holy Ghost; three Persons indeed but one essence, substance, or nature absolutely simple; the Father (proceeding) from no one, but the Son from the Father only, and the Holy Ghost equally from both, always without beginning and end. The Father begetting, the Son begotten, and the Holy Ghost proceeding; consubstantial and coequal, co-omnipotent and coeternal." [2]

The Council of Florence (1438-1445) was concerned with reconciling the Eastern and Western approaches to the intra-Trinitarian processions and emphasized that in both the Father is "the source and principle of all deity":

For when Latins and Greeks came together in this holy synod, they all strove that, among other things, the article about the procession of the holy Spirit should be discussed with the utmost care and assiduous investigation. Texts were produced from divine scriptures and many authorities of eastern and western holy doctors, some saying the holy Spirit proceeds from the Father and the Son, others saying the procession is from the Father through the Son. All were aiming at the same meaning in different words. The Greeks asserted that when they claim that the holy Spirit proceeds from the Father, they do not intend to exclude the Son; but because it seemed to them that the Latins assert that the holy Spirit proceeds from the Father and the Son as from two principles and two spirations, they refrained from saying that the holy Spirit proceeds from the Father and the Son. The Latins asserted that they say the holy Spirit proceeds from the Father and the Son not with the intention of excluding the Father from being the source and principle of all deity, that is of the Son and of the holy Spirit, nor to imply that the Son does not receive from the Father, because the holy Spirit proceeds from the Son, nor that they posit two principles or two spirations; but they assert that there is only one principle and a single spiration of the holy Spirit, as they have asserted hitherto. Since, then, one and the same meaning resulted from all this, they unanimously agreed and consented to the following holy and God-pleasing union, in the same sense and with one mind.

In the name of the holy Trinity, Father, Son and holy Spirit, we define, with the approval of this holy universal council of Florence, that the following truth of faith shall be believed and accepted by all Christians and thus shall all profess it: that the holy Spirit is eternally from the Father and the Son, and has his essence and his subsistent being from the Father together with the Son, and proceeds from both eternally as from one principle and a single spiration. We declare that when holy doctors and fathers say that the holy Spirit proceeds from the Father through the Son, this bears the sense that thereby also the Son should be signified, according to the Greeks indeed as cause, and according to the Latins as principle of the subsistence of the holy Spirit, just like the Father.

And since the Father gave to his only-begotten Son in begetting him everything the Father has, except to be the Father, so the Son has eternally from the Father, by whom he was eternally begotten, this also, namely that the holy Spirit proceeds from the Son. [3]

The Catechism promulgated by the Council of Trent (1545-1563) contemplated the "fecundity of the Father":

Let him, however, who by the divine bounty believes these truths, constantly beseech and implore God and the Father, who made all things out of nothing, and ordereth all things sweetly (Wis. 8:1), who gave us power to become the sons of God (John 1:12), and who made known to the human mind the mystery of the Trinity – let him, I say, pray unceasingly that, admitted one day into the eternal tabernacles (Luke 16:9), he may be worthy to see how great is the fecundity of the Father, who contemplating and understanding Himself, begot the Son like and equal to Himself, how a love of charity in both, entirely the same and equal, which is the Holy Ghost, proceeding from the Father and the Son, connects the begetter and the begotten by an eternal and indissoluble bond; and that thus the Essence of the Trinity is one and the distinction of the Three Persons perfect. [4]

The Church's understanding of God the Father reaches its zenith in the Second Vatican Council (1962-1965). In *Lumen Gentium*, the Council proclaims the Father as the author and director of the entire plan of creation and salvation:

The eternal Father, by a free and hidden plan of His own wisdom and goodness, created the whole world. His plan was to raise men to a participation of the divine life. Fallen in Adam, *God the Father did not leave men to themselves, but ceaselessly offered helps to salvation,* in view of Christ, the Redeemer "who is the image of the invisible God, the firstborn of every creature". All the elect, before time began, *the Father "foreknew and pre-destined to become conformed to the image of His Son,* that he should be the firstborn among many brethren". *He planned to assemble in the holy Church all those who would believe in Christ.* Already from the beginning of the world the foreshadowing of the Church took place. It was prepared in a remarkable way throughout the history of the people of Israel and by means of the Old Covenant. In the present era of time the Church was constituted and, by the outpouring of the Spirit, was made manifest. At the end of time it will gloriously achieve completion, when, as is read in the Fathers, all the just, from Adam and "from Abel, the just one, to the last of the elect," *will be gathered together with the Father in the universal Church.*

The Son, therefore, came, sent by the Father. It was in Him, before the foundation of the world, that the Father chose us and predestined us to become adopted sons, for in Him it pleased the Father to re-establish all things. To carry out the will of the Father, Christ inaugurated the Kingdom of heaven on earth and revealed to us the mystery of that kingdom. By His obedience He brought about redemption. The Church, or, in other words, the kingdom of Christ now present in mystery, grows visibly through the power of God in the world. This inauguration and this growth are both symbolized by the blood and water which flowed from the open side of a crucified Jesus, and are foretold in the words of the Lord referring to His death on the Cross: "And I, if I be lifted up from the earth, will draw all things to myself". As often as the sacrifice of the cross in which Christ our Passover was sacrificed, is celebrated on the altar, the work of our redemption is carried on, and, in the sacrament of the eucharistic bread, the unity of all believers who form one body in Christ is both expressed and brought about. All men are called to this union with Christ, who is the light of the world, from whom we go forth, through whom we live, and toward whom our whole life strains.

When the work which the Father gave the Son to do on earth was accomplished, the Holy Spirit was sent on the day of Pentecost in order that He might continually sanctify the Church, and thus, all those who believe would have access through Christ in one Spirit to the Father. He is the Spirit of Life, a fountain of water springing up to life eternal.) To men, dead in sin, the Father gives life through Him, until, in Christ, He brings to life their mortal bodies. The Spirit dwells in the Church and in the hearts of the faithful, as in a temple. In them He prays on their behalf and bears witness to the fact that they are adopted sons. The Church, which the Spirit guides in way of all truth and which He unified in communion and in works of ministry, He both equips and directs with hierarchical and charismatic gifts and adorns with His fruits. By the power of the Gospel He makes the Church keep the freshness of youth. Uninterruptedly He renews it and leads it to perfect union with its Spouse. The Spirit and the Bride both say to Jesus, the Lord, "Come!"

Thus, the Church has been seen as 'a people made one with the unity of the Father, the Son and the Holy Spirit.' …

In this way the Church both prays and labors in order that the entire world may become the People of God, the Body of the Lord and the Temple of the Holy Spirit, and *that in Christ, the Head of all, all honor and glory may be rendered to the Creator and Father of the Universe. … Christ, becoming obedient even unto death and because of this exalted by the Father*, entered into the glory of His kingdom. To Him all things are made subject until *He subjects Himself and all created things to the Father that God may be all in all.* [5]

With this dramatic declaration, the Council has drawn the attention of the faithful to the scriptural and theological foundations underlying the institution of a feast celebrating the primordial role of the Father in salvation history.

#5 PAPAL

The pontificates of St. John Paul II, Benedict XVI and Francis have focused more on the role of the Father than any other pontificates in history. They might well be called the Patriarchal Pontificates.

Their profound meditations on God the Father continue the path of development advanced by *Lumen Gentium.*

Pope St. John Paul II

"Starting with the Son, New Testament reflection and the theology based on it have plumbed the mystery of God's "fatherhood". It is the Father who is the absolute principle in Trinitarian life, the one who has no origin and from whom the divine life flows. The unity of the three Persons is a sharing in the one divine essence, but in the dynamism of reciprocal relations that have their source and foundation in the Father."[1]

"The whole of the Christian life is like a great pilgrimage to the house of the Father, whose unconditional love for every human creature, especially for the "prodigal son", we discover anew each day."[2]

Pope Benedict XVI

"God in being Father has two dimensions. First of all God is our Father because he is our Creator. Each one of us, each man and each woman, is a miracle of God, is wanted by him and is personally known by him. … Nonetheless this is still not enough. The Spirit of Christ opens us to a second dimension of God's fatherhood, beyond creation, since Jesus is the "Son" in the full sense of "one in being with the Father", as we profess in the Creed. Becoming a human being like us, with his Incarnation, death and Resurrection, Jesus in his turn accepts us in his humanity and even in his being Son, so that we too may enter into his specific belonging to God. …It is this fundamental reality that is disclosed to us when we open ourselves to the Holy Spirit and he makes us turn to God saying "Abba!", Father."[3]

"God is our Father, giving us his Son; God is our Father, pardoning our sin and bringing us to joy in everlasting life; God is our Father, giving us the Spirit that makes us sons and enables us to call him, in truth "Abba, Father!" (cf. Rom 8:15). It is for this reason that Jesus, teaching us to pray, invites us to say "Our Father" (Mt 6:9-13; cf. Lk 11:2-4). Consequently God's fatherhood is infinite love, tenderness that bends over us, frail children, in need of everything."[4]

"The Spirit is also the energy which transforms the heart of the ecclesial community, so that it becomes a witness before the world to the love of the Father, who wishes to make humanity a single family in his Son."[5]

Pope Francis

[Pope Francis opens the papal bull *Misericordiae Vultus (The Face of Mercy)* with the announcement that "Jesus Christ is the face of the Father's mercy." "Merciful like the Father" was the motto he chose for the extraordinary Jubilee Year of Mercy in 2015.]

"Calling God by the name 'Father' is not something that can be taken for granted. We are tempted to use the highest titles, which are respectful of his transcendence. But calling him 'Father' puts us in His confidence, like a child talking to his dad, knowing that he is loved and cared for by him." "God is a Father in his own way: good, helpless before man's free will, only able to conjugate the verb 'to love'."[6]

"The first step of every Christian prayer is the entry into a mystery, that of the *fatherhood of God.* … Either you enter into the mystery, in the awareness that God is your Father, or you do not pray. … The hunger for love that we all feel is not a yearning for something nonexistent: it is instead an invitation to know God who is father."[7]

"We can say that Christian prayer arises from the courage to address God with the name 'Father'. This to say 'Father' to God. But it takes courage! It is not so much a matter of a formula, as much as a filial intimacy into which we are introduced by grace: Jesus is the revealer of the Father and he gives us intimacy with him."[8]

#6 THEOLOGICAL

Theologically, as shown by *Lumen Gentium*, it is clear that the blueprint of creation and salvation originates with the Father.

The whole Bible is a story of humanity turning away from the Father and then returning to Him. The Father seeks us out through the patriarchs and the prophets, the apostles and the evangelists, and ultimately through the Son and the Spirit. The fundamental theme is the Father's love for us. "God so loved the world that he gave his only Son, so that everyone who believes in him might not perish but might have eternal life." (*John* 3:16) "God is love. In this way the love of God was revealed to us: God sent his only Son into the world so that we might have life through him. In this is love: not that we have loved God, but that he loved us and sent his Son as expiation for our sins." (1 *John* 4:8-10)

Jesus came so that we might know the Father, come to the Father and become children of the Father.

"No one knows the Father except the Son and anyone to whom the Son wishes to reveal him." *Matthew* (11:27)

"No one comes to the Father except through me.'" (*John* 14:6)

"See what love the Father has bestowed on us that we may be called the children of God." (1 *John* 3:1)

"That you may be children of your heavenly Father." (*Matthew* 5:45)

It is through the Holy Spirit that we become children of Abba our Father:

"As proof that you are children, God sent the Spirit of his Son into our hearts, crying out, 'Abba, Father!'" (*Galatians* 4:6)

"For those who are led by the Spirit of God are children of God. … You received a spirit of adoption, through which we cry, "Abba, Father!" (*Romans* 8:14-15)

The Father cannot be considered other than in relation to Son and Spirit. From all eternity, the Father gives all he is to the Son, the Son receives all he is from the Father and their common love "breathes" forth the Spirit.

In the New Testament, the Baptism of Jesus and his Transfiguration involve direct messages of the Father. In fact, the Transfiguration is celebrated as a feast of the Father by the Ethiopian Orthodox Church.

But, despite the scriptural data, we do not have a theology of the Father comparable to Christology or Pneumatology. Galot writes,

The theology of God the Father is far less developed than the theology of Christ and the theology of the Holy Spirit. It is significant that while the terms 'Christology' and 'Pneumatology' are increased used to designate doctrinal elaborations related to Christ and the Holy Spirit, we have no term that specifically denotes the doctrine relating to God the Father. …

The definition of the incarnate Son implies a distinction between the divine person of the Son and the divine person of the Father. This opens the way to a wide-ranging theological perspective in which the Father is envisioned and studied more thoroughly in his own distinct personality….

The experience of the earthly life of the incarnate Son is the point of departure for the theology of the Father. This theology must strive to explicate everything that is implied in the invocation 'Abba' and to translate in a doctrinal pronouncement the way Jesus perceived the Father and approached him in his dialogue.

The theology of the Father has its origins in Jesus' experience. But it also results from the filial experience to which all Christians are invited. The name 'Abba' must be taken seriously. It cannot consist in the mere repetition of an invocation, but must signify a profound awareness of relationship with the Father and a desire to know him better. …

Indeed we can well wonder whether the lack of progress in the theology of the Father does not stem essentially from the lack of a filial attitude in Christian life. Theology reflects life. …

The name 'Abba' that enthralled the first Christians has become a memory recorded in the letters of Paul, a testimony from the past that is too little echoed or shared in by the prayer of Christians today. Of course, the awareness of having a true Father in heaven has never been absent from the Christian psyche. However, it is not as keen as the Gospel revelation would demand.

A deepening of this awareness would strengthen the desire to discover the Father and stimulate efforts to know his divine person at greater depth. It would encourage the elaboration of a theology of the Father bound up with the specifically Christian personality, the personality of a son or daughter of the Father.[1]

Despite the lack of theological advancement, at the very minimum we need to acknowledge the Father's role in salvation.

"Precisely, because He is the initiator of all the work of salvation and the ultimate end of the journey of redeemed humanity, the Father should be celebrated," says Galot. "The liturgy must follow the essential movement which characterizes the journey and the worship of Christ, which goes from the Father to the Father."[2]

#7 ANTHROPOLOGICAL

Two anthropological concepts fundamental to modern society – the concepts of the person and of the nuclear family – arose from the affirmations of Christian theology, from "faith seeking understanding." We are now on the verge of yet another anthropological breakthrough drawn from our deeper understanding of God as Father.

The concept of the person was a fruit of the Councils that articulated the doctrine of the Trinity. "Our concept of a person was forged by the theological controversies about the Trinity," writes the logician Peter Geach.[1] The idea of the nuclear family has been correlated with devotion to the Holy Family. "Until around the beginning of the seventeenth century … the word 'family' was used in the sense of 'household' and referred to all the people under the authority of the head of the house, including relatives and servants. … During the first part of the seventeenth century, growing attention was given to the family of Jesus, Mary and Joseph. … In the first half of the seventeenth century, people began to look to Nazareth for lessons on living family life."[2]

Much like these advances, the declaration of a feast of God the Father will have a revolutionary impact on modern society given contemporary confusion about the very structure of human existence. Sterile debates about transgenderism and transhumanism, the ongoing breakdown of family and sexual ecosystems and the dismissal of Christianity as a system of patriarchal hegemony are rooted in foundational misconceptions with destructive consequences. A return to the true meaning and implications of the revelation of God as *Abba* – celebrated in a feast – will take us beyond fruitless polemics to a dynamic new vision for the future with spiritual and social benefits.

The time is ripe for the feast because modern thinkers have helped separate the transcendent truths underlying the revelation of God the Father from conventional thought-patterns that have obscured its explosive paradigm-shifting nature. The idea of God as Father has nothing to do with gender – since the infinite-eternal Spirit has no gender – and everything to do with "kinship" between the Creator and its creatures. All kinship is expressed in familial terms. It also tells us that "relationship" lies at the heart of existence – we are not atomistic individuals but born in, through and for relationship. Finally, our own families and indeed the human family are meant to mirror the Family that is God. The names we use in the human family – as in the divine Family – are concerned with the roles we play (father, mother, child), each with its unique dignity, not with notions of superiority and inferiority ("For through faith you are all children of God in Christ Jesus. ... There is neither Jew nor Greek, there is neither slave nor free person, there is not male and female; for you are all one in Christ Jesus." *Galatians* 3:26,28).

These are the breakthroughs that will be crystallized in a feast of God the Father.

Cambridge theologian Janet Soskice Smith, a feminist, rightly points out, "We cannot, without textual irresponsibility, simply go through the New Testament and replace every reference to God as "Father" with "Mother," or supplement every reference to "son" and "brother" with "daughter" and "sister". ... Biblical authors use many gendered terms, not because they are interested in sex but because they are very interested in kinship and kinship terms which, in most natural languages, are gendered. Kinship titles are titles of intimacy, of blood relation. ... The text both gives and takes away, for it is on the face of it preposterous that we, creatures, should be the kin of God. ... Kinship titles are mutually implying — if I am your kin then you are mine. Once one has a brother or a sister one is a brother or a sister. ... To claim that God is our Father, or Christ our brother, is thus to make a strong claim not only about God but about ourselves. ... We — all humanity and perhaps all 'flesh' — have become 'the kin of Christ', a family of 'first born sons.'"[3]

On the same lines, the hermeneutic phenomenologist Paul Ricoeur says, "The audacity [of addressing God as *Abba*] is possible because a new time has begun. ... Far, therefore, from the addressing of God as father being easy, along the lines of a relapse into archaism, it is rare, difficult and audacious, because it is prophetic, directed toward fulfillment rather than toward origins. It does not look backward toward a great ancestor, but forward, in the direction of a new intimacy on the model of the knowledge of the son. ... There is a father because there is a family, and not the reverse."[4]

Psychologist Paul Vitz explains why the recognition of God as Father is essential for healthy male and female identity:

Our primary concern here is with the psychological significance of the concept of the fatherhood of God. To set a context for this we address the major interpretations or models of sexuality. Probably the most familiar model of sexuality is the exploitive model in which men have traditionally dominated and taken advantage of women. This model has been rightly criticized, especially by feminists. ... I will call this the exploitation model. Throughout the world, men have dominated and exploited women in all societies of which we have any historical record. ...

The second model is what has already been termed the androgyny or unisex model. This is an understanding of sexuality as basically arbitrary, and of male and female as not only equivalent but as more or less interchangeable, except for minor differences in external genitalia and associated sensory pleasure. ...But the logic that relativizes sex to each individual also relativizes power to the individual. That is, power can now be utilized in the service of pleasure with no more restraints as well. In short, if you have the power, you can get away with sexual exploitation. ...In the androgynous situation exploitation exists in a philosophical vacuum in which anything goes. ...

The third model, which I believe to be the traditional Christian model, will be called the complementary model. Here, maleness and femaleness are seen as important and positive differences, and as fundamental to reality and to the nature of each person. God created us, male and female, and it was good. This emphasis on the reality and importance of sexual differences contrasts with androgyny. Masculinity and femininity—maleness and femaleness— are seen as cooperating in a mutually supportive fashion. This also contrasts with the exploitive model. ... What I will try to show now is how the psychological significance of the fatherhood of God helps to maintain the complementary understanding of the sexes, for both men and women. ...

The answer to macho psychology, provided by God the Father, is shown in the life of Jesus. The style of Jesus has been well described as servant leadership. ... Servant leadership is the only model I know of that is strong enough to remove the sin of male exploitive psychology. God the Father figures into this explicitly in Scripture. ...

The basic point of the Christian model of God as Father is that it allows a boy to identify strongly and positively with masculine ways of life but removes the sting of selfishness—of what psychologists call narcissism—by placing male abilities in the service of others. ... God the Father ... gives men a model with which to identify, even if their own fathers have been inadequate. Thus, the model of God the Father is a fundamental psychological support for this essential masculine need. ...

How does the fatherhood of God enhance feminine identity? I believe that it is analogous to the way in which, through love and support, a good father enhances the sexual identity of his own daughters. Much research has shown that girls raised without fathers tend to be less sure of their lovability and femininity. ... And as far as a woman's identity goes, how can she doubt her femininity, her womanhood, if it is acknowledged and honored directly through the love of God, her Father?[5]

In talking of the first Person of the Trinity as Father, we are using both metaphorical (accidental) and proper (essential) analogy. Moral theologian Benedict Ashley observes that in comparing God's creative act and the human male's role in procreation "the analogy is merely metaphorical, since impregnation is intrinsic to the human male, but not to God who creates ex nihilo, and therefore the resemblance is merely extrinsic and accidental. But if we abstract from the dependence in reproduction of the human male on the human female he impregnates and use the term 'Father' as an analogy to the God who creates out of nothing, we are using an analogy that is proper, since the point of comparison (active agency) is essential and intrinsic both to the human father and the Divine Father, although of very different types....The term 'Father' used of God in no way implies that he is male, but only that as our father gave us life and loves and cares for us, so does God." Ashley adds that the term "Father" is appropriate "within" the Trinity because we are NOT trying here to make an analogy between a "human father" as "efficient cause of his child" and God as "the efficient cause of the universe." Rather, we are saying that "As the human father is principle of his child, so the First Person, God the Father, is the principle of the Second Person, God the Son."[6]

A feast of the Father will also highlight the vital importance of the Trinity to our understanding of the family. Popes St. John Paul II, Benedict XVI and Francis have all spoken of the family itself as made in the image of the Trinity.

John Paul wrote that "Humanity images God in the family."[7] This is because "God in his deepest mystery is not a solitude but a family, since he has in himself fatherhood, sonship and the essence of the family which is love."[8] Benedict said, "Among the different analogies of the ineffable mystery of the Triune God that believers are able to discern, I would like to cite that of the family. It is called to be a community of love and life where differences must contribute to forming a 'parable of communion.'"[9] According to Francis, "God is a 'family' of three Persons who love each other so much as to form into one."[10]

Cardinal Joseph Ratzinger, later to become Benedict XVI, warned, however, that the loss of fatherhood and motherhood is among the greatest threats of our time: God himself "willed to manifest and describe himself as Father. ... Human fatherhood gives us an anticipation of what He is. But when this fatherhood does not exist, when it is experienced only as a biological phenomenon, without its human and spiritual dimension, all statements about God the Father are empty. The crisis of fatherhood we are living today is an element, perhaps the most important, threatening man in his humanity. The dissolution of fatherhood and motherhood is linked to the dissolution of our being sons and daughters."[11]

Benedict XV instituted the feast of the Holy Family in 1921 after affirming in *Bonum Sane* that "the future of society depends on the family" and "imitation of the Holy Family is the primary means to strengthen family life." It was this feast that helped establish a universal devotion to the Holy Family.

By the same token, in the present crisis, the institution of a feast of the Father would restore and regenerate fatherhood, motherhood and the family to an unprecedented degree. It is significant in terms of both theology and anthropology.

#8 MILLENNIAL

Given the momentum at the biblical, liturgical, patristic, conciliar, papal, theological and anthropological levels, perhaps we have reached the "fullness of time" for a feast for *Abba*, Father of the Human Family.

The first Christian millennium was a time when we deepened our knowledge of the Son. In the second millennium we came to a greater understanding of the Spirit. Now, in this third millennium, we are ready to know, love and honor more fully the Father from Whom all things come. The most appropriate way to commence this effort would be to institute a feast for the Father. As Cantalamessa noted, "Feasts are the highest and most solemn form of proclaiming one's faith, because all people participate in it unanimously."

Pope Leo XIII had consecrated the world to the Sacred Heart of Jesus in 1899. Popes Pius XII (1942), St. Paul VI (1964) and St. John Paul II (1984) consecrated the world to the Immaculate Heart of Mary. Pope Francis specifically consecrated Russia and Ukraine to the Immaculate Heart of Mary in 2022.

The Church also consecrates specific time periods. Pius XII (1954) and St. John Paul II (1987-88) declared Marian years. Francis proclaimed 2015-2016 as the Holy Year of Mercy and 2020-2021 as the Year of St. Joseph. In preparation for the Jubilee Year of 2000, St. John Paul II had proclaimed 1997 as the Year of

Jesus Christ, the Word of God; 1998 as the Year of the Holy Spirit; and 1999 as the Year of the Father. The Year of the Father was intended for believers to see everything *in the perspective of the "Father who is in heaven:* (cf. Mt 5:45), from whom the Lord was sent and to whom he has returned (cf. Jn 16:28)."

Also noteworthy is Leo XIII's consecration of the 20th century to the Holy Spirit at the urging of Blessed Elena Guerra (approved now for canonization): "In her ninth letter to the Pope on October 15, 1900, Elena begged him to exhort all Catholics to pray for the new century and to place it under the sign of the Holy Spirit. "Most Holy Father, I humbly present with confidence to your Holiness that the new century may begin with the hymn Veni Creator Spiritus to be sung at the beginning of the Mass of the first day of the year." And on January 1, 1901, the first day of the first year in the twentieth century, Pope Leo intoned the Veni Creator Spiritus in the name of the whole Church."[1]

And it is well known that Pope St. John XXIII called for an outpouring of the Spirit in his prayer at the opening of the Second Vatican Council: "Renew Your wonders in this our day, as by a new Pentecost." (Coincidentally, it was St. John XXIII who beatified Sr. Elena Guerra calling her an "Apostle of the Holy Spirit.")

Both papal invocations of the Holy Spirit resulted in a greater awareness of the role of the Holy Spirit across the Christian world of the 20th century.

Now as we enter not just a new century but a new millennium, we are given an opportunity to discover the Father in all his fullness.

The year-by-year calendar laid out for the Jubilee year of 2000 – the Year of the Son, then the Holy Spirit and, finally, the Father – may be seen to have a counterpart in the three Christian millennia.

We "discovered" the full identity of the Son in the first millennium through its Seven Ecumenical Councils, in the second we came to recognize the action of the Holy Spirit and now, in the third millennium, we have the opportunity to acknowledge the

Father's role in salvation history by celebrating a Feast in his honor and consecrating the world to him.

This consecration of the world to the Father is appropriate given Pope Leo XIII's consecration of the world to the Son (1899) and then to the Holy Spirit (1901). Such a consecration to the Father would complete the Trinitarian sequence.

#9 ECUMENICAL

Christmas, Easter and Pentecost are the three feasts celebrated by Christians of almost every denomination. This is obviously because they concern Jesus and the Holy Spirit.

It is to be expected that, likewise, a feast for the Father will be welcomed by most Orthodox and Protestant Christians given the centrality of the Father in the New Testament narratives.

In the New Testament, the Baptism of Jesus and his Transfiguration involve direct messages from the Father. In fact, as we have seen, the Transfiguration is celebrated as a feast of the Father by the Ethiopian Orthodox Church.

Galot spotlights the ecumenical dimensions of a feast in honor of the Father:

The 'Our Father' is the ecumenical prayer par excellence. Since this prayer gathers our separated brothers together, a feast of God our Father should contribute to this same coming together. The homage rendered to the Father in such a feast could be shared in by Christians of all denominations.

Instituting a feast in honor of God our Father would certainly be a step in the direction of the reunion of Christians. This unifying role is at the heart of our veneration of God our Father: Christians cannot pray to their heavenly Father without by that very fact being more closely united among themselves of the same spiritual family. The feast would be a symbol of Christian unity and a powerful impetus toward reconciliation.

In addition, this feast could have repercussions beyond the bounds of Christianity wherever human fatherhood is held in honor. It would respond to the deep-seated aspiration that has often been manifested in many religions, the aspiration to look to God as a Father. The feast would thus disseminate the joy of finding in God, in the father of Jesus Christ, a Father for every human person.[1]

Cantalamessa points out that

Christians would certainly give great joy to the risen Lord if they were able to accomplish this project "ecumenically", that is, reaching an agreement with all the Churches who accept it in order to celebrate, with one accord, the feast of the Father on the same day.[2]

Above all, a feast for the Father would be a major milestone in meeting the objective of Christian unity set by Vatican II.

The Vatican II Decree on Ecumenism, *Unitatis Redintegratio*, says

Division openly contradicts the will of Christ, scandalizes the world, and damages the holy cause of preaching the Gospel to every creature.

But the Lord of Ages wisely and patiently follows out the plan of grace on our behalf, sinners that we are. In recent times more than ever before, He has been rousing divided Christians to remorse over their divisions and to a longing for unity. Everywhere large numbers have felt the impulse of this grace, and among our separated brethren also there increases from day to day the movement, fostered by the grace of the Holy Spirit, for the restoration of unity among all Christians. This movement toward unity is called "ecumenical." Those belong to it who invoke the Triune God and confess Jesus as Lord and Savior, doing this not merely as individuals but also as corporate bodies. …

Today, in many parts of the world, under the inspiring grace of the Holy Spirit, many efforts are being made in prayer, word and action to attain that fullness of unity which Jesus Christ desires. The Sacred Council exhorts all the Catholic faithful to recognize the signs of the times and to take an active and intelligent part in the work of ecumenism. …

The Council moreover professes its awareness that human powers and capacities cannot achieve this holy objective – the reconciling of all Christians in the unity of the one and only Church of Christ. It is because of this that the Council rests all its hope on the prayer of Christ for the Church, on our Father's love for us, and on the power of the Holy Spirit. "And hope does not disappoint, because God's love has been poured into our hearts through the Holy Spirit, who has been given to us." (*Rom.* 5, 5)[3]

The decree specifies that it is "the Lord of Ages," the Father, who "has been rousing divided Christians to remorse over their divisions and to a longing for unity." And it concludes that achieving this objective comes not from "human powers" but from

Christ's prayer for the Church, the power of the Holy Spirit and "our Father's love for us" that "has been poured into our hearts."

A feast for the Father, whom Christians of every denomination invoke in the Lord's prayer, would lend a unique impetus to their reaching a state where "they all may be one."

A feast for the Father will also mark an irrevocable milestone in inter-religious relations.

We cannot forget these moving words of *Nostra Aetate*, Vatican II's famous decree on the "Relation of the Church to Non-Christian Religions":

> From ancient times down to the present, there is found among various peoples a certain perception of that hidden power which hovers over the course of things and over the events of human history; at times some indeed have come to the recognition of a Supreme Being, or even of a Father. This perception and recognition penetrates their lives with a profound religious sense.[4]

"Even of a Father!"

Mircea Eliade, one of the most influential modern historians of religion, wrote: "The history of supreme beings whose structure is celestial is of the utmost importance for an understanding of the religious history of humanity as a whole." He rejects the reductionist approach to universal primordial ideas of God. "There is no question of naturalism here. The celestial god is not identified with the sky, for he is the same god who, creating the entire cosmos, created the sky too. This is why he is called Creator, All-powerful, Lord, Chief, Father, and the like. The celestial god is a person, not a uranian epiphany."[5]

The *Rig Veda* (1200-900 B.C.), the first major work in an Indo-European language and the holiest scripture of Hinduism, speaks of "Our father, who created and set in order and knows all forms, all worlds."[6]

Eliade writes that "The most popular prayer in the world is addressed to 'Our Father who art in heaven.' It is possible that man's earliest prayers were addressed to the same heavenly father."[7] *Nostra Aetate* draws attention to the importance of Judaism:

Since the spiritual patrimony common to Christians and Jews is thus so great, this sacred synod wants to foster and recommend that mutual understanding and respect which is the fruit, above all, of biblical and theological studies as well as of fraternal dialogues.[8]

In this context, a major recent development was an unprecedented declaration signed by over 60 prominent Orthodox Jewish rabbis from Israel, Europe and the USA: Here is the text of their widely publicized *Orthodox Rabbinic Statement on Christianity*[9]:

"To Do the Will of Our Father in Heaven: Toward a Partnership between Jews and Christians.

After nearly two millennia of mutual hostility and alienation, we Orthodox Rabbis who lead communities, institutions and seminaries in Israel, the United States and Europe recognize the historic opportunity now before us. We seek to do the will of our Father in Heaven by accepting the hand offered to us by our Christian brothers and sisters. Jews and Christians must work together as partners to address the moral challenges of our era. ... Both Jews and Christians have a common covenantal mission to perfect the world under the sovereignty of the Almighty, so that all humanity will call on His name and abominations will be removed from the earth. We understand the hesitation of both sides to affirm this truth and we call on our communities to over-come these fears in order to establish a relationship of trust and respect."

The fact that the declaration uses the title "Our Father in Heaven" as the basis of the partnership between Jews and Christians is surely significant.

Consequently, a feast for the Father declared by the Church could end up being the first Christian feast also hailed by Jews.

Granted, Judaism does not accept the revelation of God as Triune. Nevertheless, the Hebrew Bible speaks of Father, the Word/Wisdom and the Holy Spirit.

Nostra Aetate also highlights the importance of accepting the fatherhood of God in order to recognize the common brotherhood of humankind:

We cannot truly call on God, the Father of all, if we refuse to treat in a brotherly way any man, created as he is in the image of God. Man's relation to God the Father and his relation to men his brothers are so linked together that Scripture says: "He who does not love does not know God." (1 John 4:8).

The Church's teaching of this dimension of a universal broth-erhood/sisterhood arising from our common Paternity will be clear to all with the declaration of a feast of Abba our Father, the Father of the Human Family.

#10 FRUIT-FULL

All feasts bear fruits. A feast for the Father would bear exceptional kinds of fruit – a living awareness of the Holy Trinity manifested in both liturgical worship and our devotional life; a greater insight into the family as a reflection of the divine Family that is the Trinity; a new appreciation for fatherhood as springing from the Father – "the Father, from whom every family in heaven and on earth is named." (*Ephesians* 3:14-5)

In introducing *Divinum Illud Munus*, his encyclical on the Holy Spirit, Pope Leo XIII said that it addressed "the indwelling and miraculous power of the Holy Ghost; and the extent and efficiency of His action, both in the whole body of the Church and in the individual souls of its members, through the glorious abundance of His divine graces." His desire, he said, was "that, *as a result, faith may be aroused in your minds concerning the mystery of the adorable Trinity*, and especially that piety may increase and be inflamed towards the Holy Ghost, to whom especially all of us owe the grace of following the paths of truth and virtue."

Without question, a feast for the Father would have a similar impact regarding the divine Paternity and the Holy Trinity.

Today, even among Christians, there is widespread confusion about the Trinity if not outright ignorance. The theological and devotional focus of many is exclusively on Jesus; for others it is only the Holy Spirit; and yet others speak only of God with little interest in the divine Persons.

A feast of the Father would help Christians recognize the reality of the Three Persons who are the Trinity. The Heavenly Father is Father because of his eternal Son; the Son and the Holy Spirit make us children of the Father at a supernatural level. To speak of the Father is to speak in the same breath of the Son and the Holy Spirit. The truth of the Trinity will become inescapable with an introduction of a feast of the Father.

Also, it should be said that many have a deist view of God where God is distant and uninvolved. Deism eventually leads to secularism. In celebrating the Father's acts on our behalf we would be highlighting his constant involvement in our lives.

A feast of the Father, writes Galot, has a direct impact on our attitude to fatherhood and motherhood:

> The theology of the Father has great significance for human fatherhood. It shows the excellence of all fatherhood, since in God paternity is so powerful that it forms a person. The fatherhood of the Father belongs to the primordial reality of the divine mystery, and because of this it casts light on the importance of fatherhood and motherhood in human lives. It is through fatherhood and motherhood that men and women bear within themselves the likeness of the Father and participate in the nobility of parental life.[1]

THE FEAST

Scripturally, liturgically and theologically, we have seen that there are compelling grounds for instituting a feast in honor of God the Father.

But what would such a feast celebrate and why is a feast required?

The word "feast" is derived from the Latin adjective "festus" which means "joyous"or "celebratory; "related to a time of celebration."

The practice of celebrating sacred feasts originated in Old Testament Israel and was directly commanded by God. "The LORD said to Moses: Speak to the Israelites and tell them: The following are the festivals of the LORD, which you shall declare holy days. These are my festivals." (*Leviticus* 23:1-2) The feast days were primarily intended to celebrate the redemptive acts of God in the history of Israel.

We see in the Gospels that Jesus himself celebrated these feasts. "Each year his parents went to Jerusalem for the feast of Passover, and when he was twelve years old, they went up according to festival custom." (*Luke* 2:41-2) "But the Jewish feast of Tabernacles was near. ... But when his brothers had gone up to the feast, he himself also went up, not openly but [as it were] in secret." (*John* 7:2,10)

The descent of the Holy Spirit took place on the Jewish feast of Pentecost – which became the Christian feast of Pentecost (and is celebrated by the Jews as Shavuot). The Church applied the Jewish practice of celebrating feasts in its liturgical calendar. Today, Church celebrations are of three ranks: "solemnities," feasts, and memorials.

The first Christian feasts grew out of movements originating among the faithful that were then approved by the Church. Although some have said that Christmas was first celebrated during the reign of Constantine in Rome from the year 336, other sources (e.g., the *Liber Pontificalis*) indicate its celebration may have begun as early as the second century. Different regions celebrated the feast on different days until the Church set aside December 25 in the fourth century. A date for celebrating Easter was set by the Council of Nicaea in 325.

In the early centuries of the Church, different dioceses had their own feast days celebrated in their own ways. Reforms introduced by the Council of Trent led to a single Church-wide calendar. The present categories of solemnities, feasts and memorials were introduced following the Second Vatican Council. A solemnity holds the highest rank and is reserved for celebrating a mystery of faith like the Trinity or an event in the life of Jesus such as Epiphany, or for honoring the Blessed Virgin Mary, St. Joseph, or other important saints.

In general, feast days focus on events, individuals or realities that are related to our salvation. When it comes to feast days, we do not celebrate a particular attribute of a divine Person since each member of the Trinity possesses all the divine attributes. But we do speak of a divine Person as he relates to some aspect of the work of salvation.[1] Thus the Father *sends* the Son, the Son *redeems* us and the Spirit *sanctifies* us. And salvation itself is a *return* to the Father.

Christmas and Easter celebrate acts of the Son with respect to our salvation and Pentecost likewise celebrates an act of the Holy Spirit that relates to our salvation.

But what about the Father?

The Need for the Feast

Galot writes,

"The two moments – the beginning and the end – of the work of salvation express the same truth: 'God our Father', first in the fundamental intention of the work and then in its ultimate fulfillment. The first moment occurs at the origin of the history of the universe in the divine eternity that precedes creation, and the last moment likewise opens into this eternity into which the entire substance of human history is incorporated. Christ was aware during his earthly life that he came from the Father and was going to the Father (cf. Jn 13:1-3). The Church likewise must deepen her awareness of having come forth from the Father and of advancing toward him. The liturgical feast of God the Father would express this awareness with greater clarity.

"Such a feast could not be considered an ornamental devotion. It is not a superfluous manifestation of piety, but intrinsic to the liturgical cycle of which this feast is the pinnacle. If we really want to reinstate this cycle in the biblical perspective of the discourse after the Last Supper and of Pauline teaching, we will call for a more explicit proclamation of the mystery of God the Father.

"This proclamation can be celebrated throughout the liturgical year. Yet in order to have its full impact it requires a special day of solemnity reserved for it alone. The purpose of a liturgical feast is to draw attention to a particular person or mystery. The person of God the Father and the mystery of the divine fatherhood deserve more than an implicit veneration or a mere mention in other feasts. We can adequately celebrate and thank God the Father only with a special feast in his honor."[1]

Says Cantalamessa:

"It's sad that in the whole liturgical year there isn't a feast dedicated to the Father, that in the whole Missal there isn't even a votive Mass in His honour. Come to think of it, it's very strange; there are many feasts dedicated to Jesus the Son; there is a feast of the Holy Spirit; there are many feasts dedicated to Mary… There isn't a single feast dedicated to the Father, *"source and origin of all divinity"*. We could almost say that the Father, and no longer the Holy Spirit, is "the unknown divinity".

"It's true, there is the feast of the Holy Trinity, which, however, is the feast of a mystery, or a dogma and not of a person and, nevertheless, not of a single divine person. Besides, the fact that there is a feast of the Holy Family doesn't mean the Church may not feel the need to celebrate, even individually, the three persons of the Holy Family. There are even two feasts dedicated to Jesus' putative father, but there isn't a single feast dedicated to His real Father. Couldn't this be the moment to fill this gap?

"Many feasts originated in order to answer the particular needs of an era. The feast of Corpus Domini, for example, was born as a response of faith to the denial of the real presence, made by Berengario of Tours. To the threat of Jansenism, the Church responded with the feast of and devotion to the Sacred Heart, and no one will ever know how many spiritual graces this devotion produced. Today, the threat strikes the very heart of the Christian faith which is the revelation of God as Father – the "Father of our Lord Jesus Christ", as St. Paul calls Him – and, therefore, the Trinity itself. It's not a coincidence that Providence is bringing back to mind, in our days, the mystery of God's suffering, but because the Holy Spirit knows that this is the remedy needed to heal the contaminated mind of modern man, who has found, in suffering, the stumbling stone which leads him far away from God.

"In the teachings of the Church, feasts have always been a privileged means of allowing a particular mystery or event of the history of salvation to penetrate in the lives of the faithful. The knowledge and familiarity of the Holy Spirit certainly wouldn't be so strong without the feast of Pentecost. Feasts are a living catechesis and today there is an urgent need for a catechesis on the Father. Besides its catechetic value, a feast dedicated to the Father would also have, like any other feast, the value of *homologesis*, that is of a public and joyful confession of faith. In fact, feasts are the highest and most solemn form of proclaiming one's faith, because all people participate in it unanimously."[2]

A feast day for the Father would celebrate his relationship to us with regard to our salvation as our *Abba* Father who *sent* us his Son and his Spirit for our deliverance and *to whom we return*. The verse "God so loved the world" captures the nature of this relationship to the highest degree. As Father, he brought us into being and sent us his Son and his Spirit for our salvation: this is the sacred reality we celebrate. We are celebrating his relationship to us as OUR Father who "so loved" all of humanity – and not his relationship as Father within the Trinity.

Current Celebrations of the Feast

As highlighted earlier, a feast of God the Father has been celebrated officially within the Catholic Church since the 1840s. The Archdiocese of Goiânia in Brazil celebrates the Feast of the Divine Eternal Father annually. Its church of the Divine Eternal Father was officially made a Basilica during the pontificate of Benedict XVI. It is the second largest pilgrimage destination in Brazil drawing 3 million pilgrims during the Feast Day novena which begins on the last Friday of June and ends on the first Sunday of July. The current Archbishop of Goiânia was appointed by Pope Francis in 2021 and is Vice-President of the Brazilian Bishops Conference. It is significant indeed that the largest Catholic country in the world, Brazil (123 million Catholics), has a feast celebrating God the Father. The aspiration now is to institute a feast for God as Father of humankind for the entire Church.

The co-cathedral of the Archdiocese of Kharkiv- Zaporizhzhya in Ukraine is the Church of Merciful God the Father.

Also noteworthy is the fact that the Ethiopian Orthodox Church has celebrated a feast of God the Father for centuries.

Likewise, in the 17th century, there was a "solemn celebration from time immemorial of a special feast in honor of the eternal Father in the church of the Trinitarians at Tarazona in Spain. This last-mentioned feast, which drew great throngs, was set for the Fifth Sunday after Easter."

Potential Objections Addressed

The proposal for a universal feast for the Father has been made for centuries, particularly in a concerted initiative that began in

1657. The proposal was not taken up given three objections raised at that time – objections that we now see to be groundless. These were the supposed novelty of the Feast; the possibility that a celebration of one divine Person of the Trinity could lead to polytheism; and the inadvisability of a feast honoring the divine persons in themselves separate from their roles in salvation.

About these objections, Galot writes:

When today we think about the objections made against this feast, we have difficulty understanding how it can be a serious obstacle. One of the objections was based on the novelty of the feast, a novelty which could bother people and therefore it had to be discarded: the wisdom of the elders was sufficient. Accepting this objection would mean prohibiting the introduction of any new development into the liturgy. There was also the objection of the danger of recognizing a plurality of gods: a special feast dedicated to the Father could have created some confusion on the One and Triune God, giving the idea of a kind of other God, being a divine Person distinct from the others. Such an objection could be made against all the particular feasts of Christ and the Holy Spirit. In reality, the danger of polytheism doesn't exist, and the feasts of the Persons of the Trinity can be celebrated without this concern. An argument against the feast also came from the principle that liturgical feasts had to be celebrated to commemorate a particular event of the work of salvation: in the case of the Father, there is no such event. It is easy to respond that the feast of the Holy Trinity is not connected to a particular event. Moreover, the Father intervened with His supreme initiative in all the events of the saving work and He cannot be considered extraneous to the fulfilment of His divine plan of humanity's redemption. … Precisely, because He is the initiator of all the work of salvation and the ultimate end of the journey of redeemed humanity, the Father should be celebrated.[3]

Galot makes the important point that the celebration of the feast is concerned not with the Father's eternal fatherhood but with his relationship with humanity:

A liturgical feast of God the Father should not have the eternal fatherhood within the Trinity as its principal theme. Rather, such a feast should express homage to the fatherhood that the Father has deigned to assume in relation to the members of the human race, homage to his paternal love as it has been manifested in the work of salvation. This is the purpose of the praise that St. Paul offered the Father in the hymn of the Letter to the Ephesians. ... The real object of the feast, therefore, is the fatherhood of God the Father in relation to men, a fatherhood in which the eternal fatherhood is revealed. This helps us understand why the name currently proposed for the feast of God the Father is no longer, as in the petitions made in the seventeenth century, the 'feast of the eternal Father.' but the 'feast of God our Father.'[4]

Feast Day Date

When would a Feast of the Father be celebrated? Ultimately, this is a question to be answered by the Church.

We have seen that the feast of the Divine Eternal Father in Brazil is celebrated on the first Sunday of July. In Tarazona, Spain, the feast was celebrated on the Fifth Sunday after Easter. In the Ethiopian Orthodox Church the feast of the Father is celebrated in August on the feast of the Transfiguration. The Ethiopian Orthodox

Church, in fact, also has a liturgical celebration in honor of the Father on the thirteenth of each month.

In the Church, various months are traditionally associated with the saints or Jesus – March for St. Joseph, May for the Virgin Mary, June for the Sacred Heart. In this context, given the manifestation of the Father at the Transfiguration, August is a possible option for the celebration of the feast – a month that will not conflict with the Annunciation, Easter, Pentecost or Christmas.

Another advantage of an August date for the feast is the fact that it is the Eighth Month. As is well known, the eighth day was the day ordained for sacred feasts in the Old Testament. This continued even in the New Testament with the institution of the Sabbath on "Sunday" and with the Church's emphasis on octaves.

The Jewish feast of Booths/Tabernacles was held on the eighth day:

"For seven days you shall offer an oblation to the LORD, and on the eighth day you will have a declared holy day. You shall offer an oblation to the LORD. It is the festival closing. You shall do no heavy work." *Leviticus* 23:36

"On the eighth day you will hold a public assembly: you shall do no heavy work." *Numbers* 29:35

The Jewish purification ritual was on the eighth day

"On the eighth day the individual shall take two unblemished male lambs." *Leviticus* 14:10

The feast of the Dedication of the Temple was also on the eighth day.

"On this occasion Solomon and with him all Israel, a great assembly from Lebo-hamath to the Wadi of Egypt, celebrated the festival for seven days. On the eighth day they held a solemn assembly, for they had celebrated the dedication of the altar for seven days and the feast for seven days." 2 *Chronicles* 7:8-9

In Ezekiel's vision of the future, we see,

"And when these days are over, from the eighth day on, the priests shall sacrifice your burnt offerings and communion offerings on the altar. Then I will be pleased with you." *Ezekiel* 43:27.

Jesus revealed his own consecration to the Father during the Jewish eight-day feast of Dedication.

What is important, of course, is the institution of a feast honoring the Father as the Father of the human family; the determination of a specific date for the celebration can be made in consultation with liturgists, ecumenists and others.

SUMMING UP

"'In an acceptable time I heard you, and on the day of salvation I helped you.' Behold, now is a very acceptable time; behold, now is the day of salvation." (2 *Corinthians* 6:2).

Today, as never before, we are offered a unique opportunity to complete the biblical, liturgical and theological pilgrimage to the Father that began with Jesus' announcement of "the hour … when true worshipers will worship the Father in Spirit and truth." The feasts in honor of Jesus and the Holy Spirit need to be complemented by a feast in honor of the Father who sent them on the salvific mission. We can participate in Jesus' mission to "glorify" his Abba Father when we too glorify him in a feast as *our* Abba Father, the Father of the human family.

The feast would also make sense of the biblical narratives. Both Old and New Testaments are accounts of separation from God and a return to God. Once we understand that we come from the Father and that we are called to return to the Father, everything in the Bible and in our lives would fall into place.

Above all, the feast would focus attention on the most important truth of all: God's infinite, unconditional love for each one of us and the urgency of our response to his invitation. "God so loved the world that he gave his only Son, so

that no one who believes in Him would die but instead would live forever" (*John* 3:16). Even today, many think of God as an angry deity, intent only on punishing sinful humanity. This is not the infinitely loving Father revealed by Jesus, a Father who seeks out sinners to save them and sent us his own Son for our salvation. "God our savior … wills everyone to be saved and to come to knowledge of the truth," writes St. Paul (1 *Timothy* 2:3-4).

The infinite Love of the Father is what the feast is all about and why it is essential. **It is the Father's Love for us that we would discover, celebrate, commemorate and partake of most fully in the feast.**

The glorious hymn to the Father that is *Lumen Gentium* and the majestic aspirations of *Unitatis Redintegratio* and *Nostra Aetate* will find fulfillment in the proclamation of a feast in honor of the Father of our human family.

A feast that is today already celebrated in a Particular Church – the feast of the Divine Eternal Father in Brazil – can be extended to the universal Church as the feast of Abba our Father.

Galot's concluding comments in his classic work *Abba Father We Long to See Your Face* serve as a fitting bookend to the present study:

"There are sound reasons favoring the inauguration of a feast of God our Father. Above all, there is the capital importance of the Father in the work of our salvation which needs to be given greater recognition in liturgical worship. Only a feast set apart for God the Father can assure the proper veneration of his person and respond to the universal deployment of his fatherly love.

This feast would also be most relevant for our time, since it would enhance the nobility of human parenthood and throw light on problems relating to the procreation and education of children. Nor would it be lacking in ecumenical significance. [2]

The feast is specifically relevant to fatherhood, motherhood and marriage:

Human fatherhood receives its true nobility from its participation in the primordial mystery of the heavenly Father. ... This applies to motherhood as well as fatherhood, for they both stem from the supreme parenthood of God the Father. A feast of God the Father would enable the Christian liturgy to become more completely involved in family life ... A feast of God the Father would draw attention to the divine model of all fruitfulness. It would encourage the desire for fruitfulness in marriage. [2]

Finally, the feast would enable us to participate in Jesus' relationship with the Father:

This feast is therefore to be hoped for. In a more general way, should we not want the prayer of the Church to be more closely modeled on the prayer of Christ through a greater effort to address the Father? Such a way of praying would help us rediscover the spontaneity with which Jesus called his divine Father, 'Abba!'[3]

Appendix

The Proclamation of a Feast for God the Father will Change Human History

"A son honors his father, and a servant fears his master; If, then, I am a father, where is the honor due to me?" Malachi 1:6

"I will honor those who honor me." 1 Samuel 2:30

"But the hour is coming, and is now here, when true worshipers will worship the Father in Spirit and truth; and indeed the Father seeks such people to worship him." John 4:23

The Church's declaration of a Feast of God the Father of all humankind would have an incalculable impact on the world. It would change the very trajectory of human history.

Impact of the Feast on Humanity

A feast of "Abba, the Father of the Human Family" goes beyond the bounds of theological schools and systems and reaches into every human heart. It is a proclamation by God's Church that God has no favorites (*Romans* 2:11) and that the love of the Father is directed to all peoples. The feast is a monumental testimony to the world of the Father's infinite love for each and every person. It is revealed in Scripture but is too often forgotten. "For God so **loved the world** that he gave his only Son, so that everyone who believes in him might not perish but might have eternal life." (*John* 3:16). God's love is not circumscribed. It encompasses the whole world. Just the very fact of the institution of the feast will open the minds of the multitudes, for the first time, to this stupendous truth.

Thus, the feast is nothing less than an affirmation of God's infinite, unconditional love so poignantly expressed throughout Scripture. "In this is love: not that we have loved God, but that he loved us and sent his Son as expiation for our sins." (1 *John* 4:10) This love is a paternal love, the love of a Father for all of his children: "See what love the Father has bestowed on us that we may be called the children of God." (1 *John* 3:1). "Have we not all one father? Has not one God created us?" (*Malachi* 2:10) "I will be a father to you, and you shall be sons and daughters to me, says the Lord Almighty." (2 *Corinthians* 6:18) "I kneel before the Father, from whom every family in heaven and on earth is named." (*Ephesians* 3:14) The corollary to this testament of divine love is simple: "Beloved, if God so loved us, we also must love one another." (1 *John* 4:11)

In proclaiming this feast, the Church is reaching out to all of humanity – in fulfillment of the Father's plan revealed by the Son – with a message that is life-changing. You have a Father, a Father who loves you infinitely, who invites you to love him and to love all of his children, your brothers and sisters. The feast turns our hearts toward our common Father and to our being children of this same Father. The declaration of God as Father will thus resonate with all human hearts and, in time, sprinkle the dew of love and compassion on all we do. The feast sows the seeds of an era of peace.

Devotional Impact of the Feast

The institution of previous feasts has-had a quantifiable impact on the lives of the faithful. The institution of the feast of the Sacred Heart of Jesus led almost immediately to a widespread devotion to the unquenchable love of Jesus symbolized by his Heart. There are now more churches dedicated to the Sacred Heart of Jesus than to any saint or sacred title.

To be sure, a feast of the Father will have a similarly dramatic impact on the lives of the faithful.

Papal preacher Raniero Cardinal Cantalamessa observes, "In the teachings of the Church, feasts have always been a privileged means of allowing a particular mystery or event of the history of salvation to penetrate in the lives of the faithful. Feasts are a living catechesis and today there is an urgent need for a catechesis on the Father. Besides its catechetic value, a feast dedicated to the Father would also have, like any other feast, the value of *homologesis*, that is of a public and joyful confession of faith. In fact, feasts are the highest and most solemn form of proclaiming one's faith, because all people participate in them with one heart and mind."[1]

Inter-religious Impact of the Feast

But a feast of the Father goes beyond just the faithful. It is a feast that will touch the hearts of ALL, of Catholics, non-Catholic Christians, all religious believers and even non-believers.

Nostra Aetate, Vatican II's famous decree on the "Relation of the Church to Non-Christian Religions," said, "From ancient times down to the present, there is found among various peoples a certain perception of that hidden power which hovers over the course of things and over the events of human history; at times some indeed have come to the recognition of a Supreme Being, or even **of a Father**. This perception and recognition penetrates their lives with a profound religious sense."[2]

The invocation of the Father has primordial roots that manifested themselves across cultures and eras.

Mircea Eliade, one of the most influential modern historians of religion, wrote that "The most popular prayer in the world is addressed to 'Our Father who art in heaven.' It is possible that man's earliest prayers were addressed to the same heavenly father."[3]

The *Rig Veda* (1200- 900 B.C.), the first major work in an Indo-European language and the holiest scripture of Hinduism, speaks of "Our father, who created and set in order and knows all forms, all worlds."[4]

The recent widely publicized *Orthodox Rabbinic Statement on Christianity* authored by prominent Orthodox rabbis in Israel, Europe and the USA specifically invokes the Father. The statement is titled, "To Do the Will of Our Father in Heaven: Toward a Partnership between Jews and Christians" and says, "We seek to do the will of our Father in Heaven by accepting the hand offered to us by our Christian brothers and sisters. Jews and Christians must work together as partners to address the moral challenges of our era."[5]

Unlike any other Church feast, a feast in honor of the Father would thus have a profound inter-religious impact.

Ecumenical Impact of the Feast

Christmas, Easter and Pentecost are the three feasts celebrated by Christians of almost every denomination. This is obviously because they concern Jesus and the Holy Spirit.

It is to be expected that, likewise, a feast for the Father will be welcomed by most Orthodox and Protestant Christians given the centrality of the Father in the New Testament narratives. In the New Testament, the Baptism of Jesus and his Transfiguration involve direct messages from the Father.

Jean Galot spotlights this ecumenical dimension:

The 'Our Father' is the ecumenical prayer par excellence. Since this prayer gathers our separated brothers together, a feast of God our Father should contribute to this same coming together. The homage rendered to the Father in such a feast could be shared in by Christians of all denominations. Instituting a feast in honor of God our Father would certainly be a step in the direction of the reunification of Christians. This unifying role is at the heart of our veneration of God our Father: Christians cannot pray to their heavenly Father without by that very fact being more closely united among themselves in the same spiritual family. The feast would be a symbol of Christian unity and a powerful impetus toward reconciliation.[6]

Cardinal Cantalamessa points out, "Christians would certainly give great joy to the risen Lord if they were able to accomplish this project "ecumenically," that is, reaching an agreement with all the Churches who accept it in order to celebrate, with one accord, the feast of the Father on the same day."[7]

Unitatis Redintegratio, the Vatican II Decree on Ecumenism, specifies that it is "the Lord of Ages," the Father, who "has been rousing divided Christians to remorse over their divisions and to a longing for unity." And it concludes that achieving this objective comes not from "human powers" but from Christ's prayer for the Church, the power of the Holy Spirit and ""our Father's love for us" that "has been poured into our hearts."[8]

Climax of Vatican II

A feast of the Father would consummate the majestic vision of Vatican II.

The Church's understanding of God the Father reached its zenith in the Second Vatican Council (1962-1965). In *Lumen Gentium*, the Council proclaims the Father as the author and director of the entire plan of creation and salvation: "The eternal Father, by a free and hidden plan of His own wisdom and goodness, created the whole world. His plan was to raise men to a participation of the divine life. ... The Son, therefore, came, sent by the Father. It was in Him, before the foundation of the world, that the Father chose us and predestined us to become adopted sons, for in Him it pleased the Father to re-establish all things. To carry out the will of the Father, Christ inaugurated the Kingdom of heaven on earth. ... When the work which the Father gave the Son to do on earth was accomplished, the Holy Spirit was sent on the day of Pentecost in order that He might continually sanctify the Church, and thus, all those who believe would have access through Christ in one Spirit to the Father. ... Christ, becoming obedient even unto death and because of this exalted by the Father, entered into the glory of His kingdom. To Him all things are made subject until He subjects Himself and all created things to the Father that God may be all in all."[9]

Timothy Cardinal Dolan points out that "God the Father is a very important part of the Passion. Obviously, God the Son is of infinite importance in the Passion because he is the one who is going to lay down his life so that we might live forever. But this is all part of God the Father's plan to redeem us, to get us back, to save us, to turn around the tragedy of the Garden of Eden."[10]

With *Lumen Gentium*, the Council drew the attention of the faithful to the scriptural and theological foundations underlying the institution of a feast celebrating the primordial role of the Father in salvation history.

Completion of the Trinitarian Journey

The Father cannot be considered other than in relation to Son and Spirit. From all eternity, the Father gives all he is to the Son, the Son receives all he is from the Father and their common love "breathes" forth the Spirit.

Jesus came so that we might know the Father, come to the Father and become children of the Father: "No one knows the Father except the Son and anyone to whom the Son wishes to reveal him." *Matthew* (11:27) "No one comes to the Father except through me.'" (*John* 14:6)

"That you may be children of your heavenly Father." (*Matthew* 5:45)

It is through the Holy Spirit that we become children of Abba our Father: "As proof that you are children, God sent the Spirit of his Son into our hearts, crying out, 'Abba, Father!'" (*Galatians* 4:6) "For those who are led by the Spirit of God are children of God. … You received a spirit of adoption, through which we cry, "Abba, Father!" (*Romans* 8:14-15)

The movement from and to the Father reaches a crescendo in Jesus' stunning declaration in the Gospel of John: "But the hour is coming, and is now here, when true worshipers will worship the Father in Spirit and truth; and indeed the Father seeks such people to worship him." (*John* 4:23)

Jesus says "It was for this purpose that I came to this hour. Father, glorify your name." (*John* 12:27-8)

God is to be approached as Father. True worship of God is worship of the Father. The Father seeks out those who worship him in Spirit and truth. This is the God revealed by Jesus of Nazareth.

In his exegesis of *John* 4:23, Jean Galot writes,

In saying 'the hour is coming and is now' Jesus demonstrated he was aware of the times in which he was living. It was a moment of radical transformation in worship determined by God's own plan. A new age in the religious history of humankind was dawning. The era of national partisanship in worship, the time of the fathers, was over. … The time of the Father had come; it was he, the one and only Father, who laid the foundations of universality in worship and adoration. … The new worship which Jesus began consists of adoring the Father: and yet there is no day in which this adoration is directed more particularly to the person of the Father.[11]

We "discovered" the full identity of the Son in the first millennium through its Seven Ecumenical Councils, in the second we came to recognize the action of the Holy Spirit and now, in the third millennium, we have the opportunity to acknowledge the Father's role in salvation history by celebrating a Feast in his honor and consecrating the world to him.

Also appropriate would be the consecration of the world to the Father given Pope Leo XIII's consecration of the world to the Son (1899) and then to the Holy Spirit (1901). Such a consecration to the Father would be the culmination of humanity's loving surrender to the Holy Trinity.

NOTES

Summary

[1]Reinhold Schneider, *Das Vaterunser* (Freiburg: Herder, 1979), 10.

[2]Raniero Cantalamessa, *The True Lordship of Christ*, Ancora, 1990, 96-9.

[3]Jean Galot, "The new worship of the Father," December 1999.

[4]Jean Galot, *Abba Father We Long to See Your Face* (New York: Alba House, 1992), 231-2.

Biblical

[1]"This essential union with the Father not only accompanies Jesus' activity, but defines his whole being"– Pope St. John Paul II, March 10, 1999.

[2] Homily, Solemnity of Saint Joseph, Abu Dhabi, 19 March 2022 https://avosa.org/news/homily-of-cardinal-parolin-for-the-solemnity-of-st-joseph-at-abu-dhabi

[3]Jean Galot, Abba Father We Long to See Your Face (New York: Alba House, 1992), 204-5.

[4]Jean Galot, "The new worship of the Father," December 1999.

Liturgical

[1]*Catechism of the Catholic Church*, 1324.
[2]Ibid., 1359-1360.
[3]Louis Bouyer, *The Invisible Father* (Edinburgh: T&T Clark, 1999), 231.
[4]Jean Galot, "The new worship of the Father," December 1999.
[5]Raniero Cantalamessa, *The True Lordship of Christ*, Ancora, 1990, 96-9.
[6]Jean Galot, op cit.

Patristic

[1]*Adverses haereses* (5:18:2:78-79).
[2]*Four Letters to Serapion of Thmuis*, (1:28, 3:6).
[3]*Against Eunomius* (3:1).
[4]*De Trin.* IV, 20, 29 (*PL* 42, 908).
[5]Gilles Emery, *Trinity in Aquinas* (Ann Arbor, MI: Sapientia Press, 2003), 197.
[6]Louis Bouyer, *The Invisible Father* (Edinburgh: T&T Clark, 1999), 231. Bouyer goes on to say,
"But ... the very fact that God, the God of the biblical Word spoken fully in the Gospel, is Father, and a Father not accidentally but essentially, has a twofold necessary implication. Firstly, his Son, the Son, is essential to his life, his eternal subsistence as Father. Then, the Son is one with him in his term, in his eternal self-realization, just as he is in his principle or origin. This "coincidence" of the Son with the Father ... has its expression, ... its eternal realization, in that Spirit of life who proceeds from the Father at the same time as the latter begets the Son, and who rests eternally on the Son as the Gift par excellence, the Gift of self-giving."
[7]"The Father as the Source of the Whole Trinity," Augustinians of the Assumption, January 1996, 36-43. Also: https://www.catholicculture.org/culture/library/view.cfm?id=1176

Conciliar

[1]https://web.mit.edu/ocf/www/nicene_creed.html
[2]https://history.hanover.edu/courses/excerpts/344lat.html
[3]https://www.ewtn.com/catholicism/library/
ecumenical-council-of-florence-1438-1445-1461
[4]http://www.catholicapologetics.info/thechurch/catechism/
ApostlesCreed01.shtml#:~:text=The%20meaning%20of%20
the%20above,and%20not%20only%20do%20I
[5]https://www.vatican.va/archive/hist_councils/ii_vatican_council/
documents/vat-ii_const_19641121_lumen-gentium_en.html

Papal

[1]March 10, 1999.
[2]*Tertio Millennio Adveniente*, 49, November 10, 1994.
[3]May 23, 2012.
[4]January 30, 2013.
[5] *Deus Caritas Est*, "God Is Love," 2006.
[6]June 7, 2017.
[7]February 20, 2019.
[8]May 22, 2019.

Theological

[1]Jean Galot, *Abba Father We Long to See Your Face* (New York: Alba
House, 1992), 31, 37, 61, 65-6.
[2]Jean Galot, "The new worship of the Father," December 1999.

Anthropological

[1]Peter Geach, *The Virtues* (Cambridge: Cambridge University Press,
1977), 41-3

²https://www.holyfamilybordeaux.org/wp-content/uploads/2015/08/
Emergence-of-devotion-to-The-Holy-Family1.pdf
³https://hail.to/tui-motu-interislands-magazine/article/iIcHIZu
⁴Paul Ricoeur, "Fatherhood: From Phantasm to Symbol," in ed. D. Ihde,
The Conflicts of Interpretation: Essays in Hermeneutics (Evanston:
Northwestern University Press, 1974), 490-1, 479.
⁵https://www.touchstonemag.com/archives/article.
php?id=14-01-033-f&readcode=&readtherest=true#therest
⁶Benedict Ashley, O.P., *Justice in the Church: Gender and
Participation* (Washington, D.C.: The Catholic University of America
Press, 1996)107-108.
⁷John Paul II, *Letter to Families*, 6.
⁸John Paul II, *Puebla: A Pilgrimage of Faith* (Boston: Daughters of
Saint Paul, 1979), 86.
⁹https://www.vatican.va/content/benedict-xvi/en/angelus/2006/docu-
ments/hf_ben-xvi_ang_20060611.html
¹⁰May 22, 2016
¹¹ https://stmaxmedia.com/old/kolbe.html

Millennial

¹https://albanyccr.org/documents/2024/2/Flame-1-2.pdf

Ecumenical

¹Jean Galot, Abba Father We Long to See Your Face (New York:
Alba House, 1992), 231-2.
²Raniero Cantalamessa, The True Lordship of Christ, Ancora,
1990, 96-9.
³https://www.vatican.va/archive/hist_councils/ii_vatican_council/
documents/vat-ii_decree_19641121_unitatis-redintegratio_en.html
⁴https://www.vatican.va/archive/hist_councils/ii_vatican_council/
documents/vat-ii_decl_19651028_nostra-aetate_en.html

⁵Mircea Eliade, The Sacred and the Profane (New York: Harvest, 1957), 129.
⁶Rig Veda 10.82.3
⁷Mircea Eliade, Patterns in Comparative Religion trans. R. Sheed (London: Sheed & Ward Ltd., 1958), 38.
⁸https://www.vatican.va/archive/hist_councils/ii_vatican_council/documents/vat-ii_decl_19651028_nostra-aetate_en.html
⁹https://www.jcrelations.net/statements/statement/to-do-the-will-of-our-father-in-heaven-toward-a-partnership-between-jews-and-christians.html

Fruit-Full

¹Jean Galot, *Abba Father We Long to See Your Face* (New York: Alba House, 1992), 56.

The Feast

¹Jean Galot, *Abba Father We Long to See Your Face* (New York: Alba House, 1992), 226.
²Raniero Cantalamessa, *The True Lordship of Christ*, Ancora, 1990, 96-9.
³Jean Galot, "The new worship of the Father", December 1999.
⁴Jean Galot, *Abba Father We Long to See Your Face* (New York: Alba House, 1992), 211-2

Summing Up

¹Jean Galot, *Abba Father We Long to See Your Face* (New York: Alba House, 1992), 233.
²Ibid., 227-9
³Ibid., 233.

Appendix – The Proclamation of a Feast for God the Father will Change Human History

[1]Raniero Cantalamessa, The True Lordship of Christ, Ancora, 1990, 96-9.

[2]https://www.vatican.va/archive/hist_councils/ii_vatican_council/documents/vat-ii_decl_19651028_nostra-aetate_en.html

[3]Mircea Eliade, Patterns in Comparative Religion trans. R. Sheed (London: Sheed & Ward Ltd., 1958), 38.

[4]Rig Veda 10.82.3

[5]https://www.jcrelations.net/statements/statement/to-do-the-will-of-our-father-in-heaven-toward-a-partnership-between-jews-and-christians.html

[6]Jean Galot, Abba Father We Long to See Your Face (New York: Alba House, 1992), 231-2.

[7]Raniero Cantalamessa, The True Lordship of Christ, Ancora, 1990, 96-9.

[8]https://www.vatican.va/archive/hist_councils/ii_vatican_council/documents/vat-ii_decree_19641121_unitatis-redintegratio_en.html

[9]https://www.vatican.va/archive/hist_councils/ii_vatican_council/documents/vat-ii_const_19641121_lumen-gentium_en.html

[10]https://www.facebook.com/watch/?v=773441867283207

[11]Jean Galot, Abba Father We Long to See Your Face (New York: Alba House, 1992), 204-5.